Lyndon Baines Johnson
(1908 – 1973)

QUOTATIONS

OF

Lyndon Baines Johnson

APPLEWOOD BOOKS
Carlisle, Massachusetts

Lyndon Baines Johnson

LYNDON BAINES JOHNSON was born on August 27, 1908, near Stonewall, Texas. He was the eldest of five children born to Samuel Ealy Johnson Jr., a Texas legislator, and Rebekah Baines Johnson.

In school, Johnson was involved in debate, public speaking, and baseball. He was elected eleventh grade class president and, at age fifteen, was believed to be the youngest graduate of Johnson City High School.

Johnson worked various jobs before enrolling in Southwest Texas State Teachers College. His first job after starting college was as a teacher at a poor school in Cotulla, Texas. Johnson's experience there helped forge his understanding of poverty and the role of government. In 1931, he secured a job as a congressional secretary.

While Johnson was rising through the ranks in Washington, he met Claudia Alta "Lady Bird" Taylor. After a whirlwind romance, they were married in 1934. They had two daughters, Lynda Bird and Luci Baines.

Johnson was elected to the U.S. House of Representatives in 1937. During his time there he allied himself with President Franklin D. Roosevelt and other influential people. Johnson served as an officer in the Naval Reserve from late 1941 to 1942. He received the Silver Star for his actions during observation flights in the Southwest Pacific.

In 1948, Johnson was elected to the U.S.

Senate. He was elected Majority Whip in 1951. He became the youngest Minority Leader in the history of the Senate in 1953 and became Majority Leader in 1955.

In 1960, Johnson was elected Vice President. He assumed the presidency on November 22, 1963, after the assassination of President Kennedy.

Building on what he had learned in Cotulla and from Roosevelt's New Deal, he embarked on an ambitious domestic agenda. Coined "The Great Society," Johnson's initiative set off to address issues of poverty, education, crime, health care, and the environment. Johnson's Civil Rights Act of 1964 was only one of many bills aimed at making the U.S. a safer, healthier, and more just place to live.

Protests to the war and controversy surrounding Johnson had become acute by the end of March 1968. On March 31, 1968, focusing his energies on negotiating an honorable peace, he announced that he would not seek another term. Johnson died at his ranch on January 22, 1973, one day after receiving word that peace had been reached.

Johnson's last public appearance, six weeks before his death, was at a civil rights symposium held at the LBJ Library. There, civil rights activist Julian Bond spoke of Johnson, lamenting that "an activist, human-hearted man had his hand on the levers of power and a vision beyond the next election. He was there when we, and the Nation, needed him. And oh, by God, do I wish he was there now!" Americans continue to feel the impact of Johnson's Great Society in nearly every aspect of modern life.

QUOTATIONS

OF

Lyndon Baines Johnson

The right to vote is the basic right, without which all others are meaningless. It gives people — people as individuals — control over their own destinies.
– Remarks on the Senate floor, July 24, 1957

I hardly ever think of politics.... I absolutely never spend more than eighteen hours a day on the subject.
– Houston, Texas, October 22, 1959

Until justice is blind to color, until all education is unaware of race, until opportunity is unconcerned with the color of men's skins, emancipation will be a proclamation, but emancipation will not be a fact.
– Remarks at Gettysburg, May 30, 1963

*T*his is a sad time for all people. We have
suffered a loss that cannot be weighed. For me, it
is a deep personal tragedy. I know that the world
shares the sorrow that Mrs. Kennedy and her
family bear. I will do my best. That is all I can do.
I ask for your help—and God's.

– Remarks upon arrival at Andrews Air Force Base,
   November 22, 1963

*T*he greatest leader of our time has been
struck down by the foulest deed of our time.
Today John Fitzgerald Kennedy lives on in the
immortal words and works that he left behind.
He lives on in the mind and memories of
mankind. He lives on in the hearts of his
countrymen. No words are sad enough to express
our sense of loss. No words are strong enough to
express our determination to continue the
forward thrust of America that he began.

– Address to a joint session of Congress, November 27, 1963

We must be constantly prepared for the worst, and constantly acting for the best. We must be strong enough to win any war, and we must be wise enough to prevent one.

– State of the Union address, January 8, 1964

In a free land where men move freely and act freely, the right to vote freely must never be obstructed.

– Statement announcing the adoption of the Twenty-fourth Amendment to the Constitution, the White House, January 23, 1964

Our confidence that freedom will continue to spread is based not on any desire to make the world over in America's image, but it is based upon our belief that democracy is a universal hope of all humanity.

– Remarks at a Democratic dinner, Miami Beach, February 27, 1964

*T*he war on poverty is not a struggle simply to support people, to make them dependent on the generosity of others. It is a struggle to give people a chance. It is an effort to allow them to develop and use their capacities, as we have been allowed to develop and use ours, so that they can share, as others share, in the promise of this nation.

– Message to Congress, March 16, 1964

*I*n this free land, the minds of our young are our most valuable resource. The classroom teacher is always the steward of that resource.

– Remarks upon presenting the National Teacher Award, the White House, May 4, 1964

*T*homas Jefferson pointed out that no government ought to be without censors. I can assure you, where the press is free, none will ever be needed.

– Remarks at the presentation of the William Randolph Hearst Foundation Journalism Awards, the White House, May 11, 1964

*F*or in your time we have the opportunity
to move not only toward the rich society and
the powerful society, but upward to the
Great Society.

The Great Society rests on abundance and
liberty for all. It demands an end to poverty and
racial injustice, to which we are totally
committed in our time. But that is just the
beginning.

– Commencement address at the University of Michigan,
  May 22, 1964

*T*his Civil Rights Act is a challenge to all of us
to go to work in our communities and our States,
in our homes and in our hearts, to eliminate the
last vestiges of injustice in our beloved country.

– Signing of the Civil Rights Act, July 2, 1964

We believe that all men are created equal. Yet many are denied equal treatment. We believe that all men have certain unalienable rights. Yet many Americans do not enjoy those rights. We believe that all men are entitled to the blessings of liberty. Yet millions are being deprived of those blessings—not because of their own failures, but because of the color of their skin. The reasons are deeply imbedded in history and tradition and the nature of man. We can understand—without rancor or hatred—how this all happened. But it cannot continue. Our Constitution, the foundation of our Republic, forbids it. The principles of our freedom forbid it. Morality forbids it. And the law I will sign tonight forbids it.

– Signing of the Civil Rights Act, July 2, 1964

Poverty at home is an enemy of our society as much as aggressors abroad. Poverty amid plenty can subvert our prosperity and undermine our stability.

– Remarks to labor leaders, the White House, July 24, 1964

The world must never forget—that aggression unchallenged is aggression unleashed.

– Remarks at Syracuse University, August 5, 1964

The contest is the same that we have faced at every turning point in history. It is not between liberals and conservatives; it is not between party and party, or platform and platform. It is between courage and timidity. It is between those who have vision and those who see what can be, and those who want only to maintain the status quo. It is between those who welcome the future and those who turn away from its promises.

– Remarks accepting the nomination for president, Democratic National Convention, Atlantic City, August 27, 1964

*G*iving a man a chance to work and feed his family and provide for his children does not destroy his initiative. Hunger destroys initiative. Hopelessness destroys initiative. Ignorance destroys initiative. A cold and indifferent government destroys initiative.

– Remarks at the dedication of the Morgantown, West Virginia, airport, September 20, 1964

*I*t is by our deeds and not by our words that we lead the rest of the world in the cause of freedom.

– Remarks in Oklahoma City, September 25, 1964

*T*he Government has a responsibility never to waste taxpayers' money, but the Government also has a responsibility never to waste the Nation's resources. The real wasters, the real spendthrifts, are those who are neglecting the needs of today and destroying the hopes of tomorrow.

– Remarks at the dedication of the Eufaula Dam, Eufaula, Oklahoma, September 25, 1964

*T*hree things—and three things only—sustain life on this planet. They are: a thin layer of soil, a cover of atmosphere, and a little rainfall. This is all that the good Lord has given us. Except one thing: He has given us a choice of what we will do with it. We can waste it. We can pollute it. We can neglect it. Or we can conserve it, and we can protect it, and we can develop it, and we can pass it along to our children, more promising, more abundant than we found it when we discovered America.

– Remarks at the dedication of the Eufaula Dam, Eufaula, Oklahoma, September 25, 1964

*I*f we turn away from knowledge and truth, we will not succeed…. But if we are courageous and farsighted and farseeing, if we have no fear of the truth, if we seek only after light, then we and our children and our children's children shall know the greatness of this wonderful, beautiful land we call America.

– Remarks at the 200th-anniversary convocation of Brown University, Providence, Rhode Island, September 28, 1964

Concern yourselves not with what seems feasible, not with what seems attainable, not with what seems politic, but concern yourselves with only what you know is right.

– Remarks at the 200th-anniversary convocation of Brown University, Providence, Rhode Island, September 28, 1964

The American people want leadership which believes in them, not leadership which berates them.

– Remarks at Bergen, New Jersey, October 14, 1964

True courage in this nuclear age lies in the steadfast pursuit of peace, whatever the setbacks, whatever the difficulties, however long the journey.

– Remarks at a rally, Jacksonville, Florida, October 26, 1964

There are no problems which we cannot solve together, and there are very few which any of us can settle by himself.

– News conference at the LBJ Ranch near Stonewall, Texas,
  November 28, 1964

The opportunity we give to the arts is a measure of the quality of our civilization.

– Groundbreaking ceremony for the John F. Kennedy Center for the
  Performing Arts, Washington, December 2, 1964

Our own freedom and growth have never been the final goal of the American dream. We were never meant to be an oasis of liberty and abundance in a worldwide desert of disappointed dreams. Our Nation was created to help strike away the chains of ignorance and misery and tyranny wherever they keep man less than God means him to be.

– State of the Union address, January 4, 1965

*T*he Great Society asks not how much, but how good; not only how to create wealth but how to use it; not only how fast we are going, but where we are headed. It proposes as the first test for a nation: the quality of its people.

– State of the Union address, January 4, 1965

A President's hardest task is not to do what is right, but to know what is right.

– State of the Union address, January 4, 1965

*O*ver the years the ancestors of all of us— some 42 million human beings—have migrated to these shores. The fundamental, longtime American attitude has been to ask not where a person comes from but what are his personal qualities. On this basis men and women migrated from every quarter of the globe. By their hard work and their enormously varied talents they hewed a great nation out of a wilderness. By their dedication to liberty and equality, they created a society reflecting man's most cherished ideals.

–Message to Congress, January 13, 1965

Quotations of Lyndon Baines Johnson

The war against poverty is, in the last
analysis, the struggle for human decency
and independence.

– Statement on the nation's first Neighborhood Youth Corps project,
  February 14, 1965

From the very beginning, this country, the idea
of America itself, was the promise that all would
have an equal chance to share in the fruits of our
society…. Not meanly or grudgingly, but in
obedience to an old and generous faith, let us
make a place for all at the table of American
abundance.

– Letter to the President of the Senate and Speaker of the House on
  stepping up the war on poverty, February 17, 1965

The women of America represent a reservoir
of talent that is still underused. It is too often
underpaid, and almost always under-promoted.

– Remarks at the Federal Woman's Award ceremony, the White
  House, March 2, 1965

The promise of America is a simple promise:
Every person shall share in the blessings of this
land. And they shall share on the basis of their
merits as a person. They shall not be judged by
their color or by their beliefs, or by their religion,
or by where they were born, or the neighborhood
in which they live.

– Remarks at a news conference, the White House, March 13, 1965

There is no moral issue. It is wrong—deadly
wrong—to deny any of your fellow Americans
the right to vote in this country. There is no issue
of States rights or national rights. There is only
the struggle for human rights.

– Special address to Congress, March 15, 1965

Their cause must be our cause too. Because it is
not just Negroes, but really it is all of us, who
must overcome the crippling legacy of bigotry
and injustice. And we shall overcome.

– Special address to Congress, March 15, 1965

Our mission is at once the oldest and the most basic of this country: to right wrong, to do justice, to serve man.
– Special address to Congress, March 15, 1965

People cannot contribute to the Nation if they are never taught to read or write, if their bodies are stunted from hunger, if their sickness goes untended, if their life is spent in hopeless poverty just drawing a welfare check.
– Special address to Congress, March 15, 1965

My first job after college was as a teacher in Cotulla, Texas, in a small Mexican-American school…. Somehow you never forget what poverty and hatred can do when you see its scars on the hopeful face of a young child…. It never even occurred to me in my fondest dreams that I might have the chance to help the sons and daughters of those students, and to help people like them all over this country. But now I do have that chance—and I'll let you in on a secret—I mean to use it.
– Special address to Congress, March 15, 1965

*T*o deny a man his hopes because of his color or race, his religion or the place of his birth is not only to do injustice, it is to deny America and to dishonor the dead who gave their lives for American freedom.

– Special address to Congress, March 15, 1965

*T*he real hero of this struggle is the American Negro. His actions and protests, his courage to risk safety and even to risk his life, have awakened the conscience of this nation. His demonstrations have been designed to call attention to injustice, designed to provoke change, designed to stir reform. He has called upon us to make good the promise of America. And who among us can say that we would have made the same progress were it not for his persistent bravery, and his faith in American democracy.

– Special address to Congress, March 15, 1965

I want to be the President who educated young
children to the wonders of their world. I want to
be the President who helped feed the hungry and
to prepare them to be taxpayers instead of tax
eaters. I want to be the President who helped the
poor to find their own way and who protected
the right of every citizen to vote in every
election. I want to be the President who helped
to end hatred among his fellow men and who
promoted love among the people of all races and
religions and all parties.

– Special address to Congress, March 15, 1965

*T*his is one Nation. What happens in Selma or
in Cincinnati is a matter of legitimate concern to
every American. But let each of us look within
our own hearts and our own communities, and
let each of us put our shoulder to the wheel to
root out injustice wherever it exists.

– Special address to Congress, March 15, 1965

We often say how impressive power is. But I do not find it impressive at all. The guns and the bombs, the rockets and the warships are all symbols of human failure. They are necessary symbols. They protect what we cherish. But they are witness to human folly.

– Address at Johns Hopkins University, Baltimore, April 7, 1965

In a free society, skepticism toward government is both healthy and imperative and we should welcome it, but private citizens should always guard against allowing such healthy skepticism to corrode or to destroy their respect for their fellow citizens who serve them.

– Remarks at the presentation of the President's Award for Distinguished Federal Civilian Service, the White House, June 2, 1965

Man's most noble enterprise is the work of education. In our Nation's classrooms, our future is being built. I believe that the chief architects of that future are the teachers of America.

– Remarks on the proposed teaching professions bill, the White House, July 17, 1965

*N*o longer will older Americans be denied the healing miracle of modern medicine. No longer will illness crush and destroy the savings that they have so carefully put away over a lifetime so that they might enjoy dignity in their later years. No longer will young families see their own incomes, and their own hopes, eaten away simply because they are carrying out their deep moral obligations. And no longer will this Nation refuse the hand of justice to those who have given a lifetime of service and wisdom and labor to the progress of this progressive country.

– Remarks at the signing of the Medicare Act, July 30, 1965

*T*here is no sane description of a nuclear war. There is only the blinding light of man's failure to reason with his fellow man and then silence.

– Statement on the draft Treaty to Prevent the Spread of Nuclear Weapons, August 17, 1965

*A*rt is a nation's most precious heritage. For it is in our works of art that we reveal to ourselves, and to others, the inner vision which guides us as a nation. And where there is no vision, the people perish.

– Signing of the Arts and Humanities Act, the White House,
September 29, 1965

*W*hen the earliest settlers poured into a wild continent there was no one to ask them where they came from. The only question was: Were they sturdy enough to make the journey, were they strong enough to clear the land, were they enduring enough to make a home for freedom, and were they brave enough to die for liberty if it became necessary to do so?

And so it has been through all the great and testing moments of American history. Our history this year we see in Vietnam. Men there are dying—men named Fernandez and Zajac and Zelinko and Mariano and McCormick. Neither the enemy who killed them nor the people whose independence they have fought to save ever asked them where they or their parents came from. They were all Americans.

– Remarks at the signing of the Immigration Bill, Liberty Island,
New York, October 3, 1965

I shall never forget the faces of the boys and the girls in that little Welhausen Mexican School, and I remember even yet the pain of realizing and knowing then that college was closed to practically every one of those children because they were too poor. And I think it was then that I made up my mind that this nation could never rest while the door to knowledge remained closed to any American.

– Remarks at Southwest Texas State College upon signing the Higher Education Act of 1965, November 8, 1965

*A*merica's greatness is guaranteeing to every child all the education that he or she can take. America's greatness is bringing the miracle of modern medicine to every humble citizen of this land. America's greatness is equality of race, respect of religion, and blindness of color. America's greatness is food for hungry people. America's greatness is the helping hand to the child of the slum. America's greatness is training for the unemployed. America's greatness is willingness to lend a helping hand to our neighbors from other lands who seek freedom here in our shores.

– Remarks in San Antonio at a reception honoring Representative Henry Gonzalez, November 21, 1965

*P*eace is not merely the absence of war. It is that climate in which man may be liberated from the hopelessness that imprisons his spirit.

– Remarks at the lighting of the nation's Christmas tree, the White House, December 17, 1965

*O*ur democracy cannot remain static, a prisoner to the past, if it is to enrich the lives of coming generations. Laws and institutions—to paraphrase Jefferson—must go hand in hand with the progress of the human mind, and must respond to the changing conditions of life itself.

– Message to Congress, January 20, 1966

*S*ocial injustice is not the sole reason for crime. Social justice is not the sole cure.... The vast majority of our citizens who suffer poverty and discrimination do not turn to crime. But where legitimate opportunities are closed, illegitimate opportunities are seized. Whatever opens opportunity and hopes will help to prevent crime and foster responsibility.

– Message to Congress, March 9, 1966

*T*he United States was born in strife and it was nurtured in hardship.... We have not come this long distance in history because we were a weak or a frightened or a fearful or a timid people. When America grows afraid and loses its commitment to freedom, that is the day that America will begin to die.

– Remarks upon arrival at the airport, Lawrenceville, Illinois,
   July 23, 1966

*P*overty. There is the real enemy. Strike poverty down tonight and much of the crime will fall down with it.

– Remarks to the delegates to the Conference of State
   Committees on Criminal Administration, University of Maryland,
   October 15, 1966

I say to the leaders in Hanoi: Let us lay aside our arms and sit down together at the table of reason. Let us renounce the works of death—and take up, instead, the tasks of the living. Enough of this sorrow. Let us begin the work of healing, of teaching, of building, and of providing for the children of men. This is the purpose for which we were really made; this is what our age asks us to do.

– Remarks at Chulalongkorn University, Bangkok, Thailand, October
   29, 1966

*I*t is no part of America's dream that we should erect a house of material well-being in the cheerless atmosphere of physical blight. Our people will be denied their heritage if they must live out their lives among polluted rivers, spoiled fields and forests, and streets where nothing pleases the eye.

– Proclamation, Youth for Natural Beauty and Conservation Year, December 28, 1966

*W*hen we ask what this nation or any nation expects to find from exploration in space, the answer is one word: knowledge—knowledge we shall need to maintain Earth as a habitable environment for man.

– Message to the Senate regarding ratification of the Outer Space Treaty, February 7, 1967

*T*here is one thought that I wish I could plant in the mind of every man and woman in this country.... You can believe in America. You can believe in your country's ability to fulfill her promise to the people and to the world.

– Remarks in New York City at the New York state Democratic dinner, June 3, 1967

*T*he test before us as a people is not whether our commitments match our will and our courage, but whether we have the will and the courage to match our commitments.

– Message to Congress, August 3, 1967

*M*ost people come in to the office with great dreams, and they leave it with many satisfactions and some disappointments. As to how successful we've been in doing the greatest good for the greatest number, the people themselves, and their posterity must ultimately decide.

– The film *The President's House*, 1968

One of the great blessings that has been mine
is four quite important women in my life: my
mother, my wife, and my two daughters. All of
them counsel me and guide me and strengthen
me and support me. And, except for that, the job
would be much more lonely, and I am afraid I
would be much weaker.

– Interview with President and Mrs. Johnson on a recorded program,
A View from the White House, December 27, 1968

We have proved that great progress is possible.
We know how much still remains to be done.
And if our efforts continue, if our will is strong
and our hearts are right…I am confident we shall
overcome.

– LBJ Presidential Library Civil Rights Symposium,
December 12, 1972